CENTRO
Journal of the Center for Puerto Rican Studies
VOLUME XXXII
NUMBER III
FALL 2020

ISBN 978-1-945662-45-4

Center for Puerto Rican Studies
Hunter College / City University of New York
695 Park Avenue, E-1429,
New York, NY 10065
https://centropr.hunter.cuny.edu/publications/centro-press

Puerto Rico has suffered the compounded effects of multiple disasters since the devastating impacts of Hurricanes Irma and Maria in September 2017. At the end of 2019, the island was impacted with recurrent seismic activity in the southwest region, and in January 2020 the unset of the COVID-19 pandemic. All these disasters are underscored by a crushing debt crisis and a federally mandated austerity regime since 2016. Recent disasters have revealed serious vulnerabilities in Puerto Rico's preparedness planning, institutional response capacity and coordination, resource management at various levels of implementation, data availability, and the lack of suitable and accessible mechanisms to support adequate local community engagement. The collection of studies included in this special volume of *CENTRO Journal* show evidence of how post disaster recovery is progressing in Puerto Rico, the challenges and opportunities for local participation in reconstruction programs, and the potential of nonprofit organizations, municipalities, and local businesses to contribute to post disaster recovery in Puerto Rico. To date, the available evidence leads to a portrait of an uneven recovery. The studies included in this volume indicate that the long-term impact of post-disaster federal funding for economic recovery is contingent on implementing a comprehensive strategy for reforming public policy to encourage and support nonprofit developers' participation in reconstruction programs, building industry capacity by strengthening intermediaries and CDCs, encouraging intra-industry partnerships and collaborations, and providing professional development for economic recovery.

Special Issue: Post-Disaster Recovery in Puerto Rico and Local Participation
Guest Editor: Edwin Meléndez

VOLUME XXXII • NUMBER III • FALL 2020

Post-Disaster Recovery in Puerto Rico and Local Participation: Introduction

EDWIN MELÉNDEZ

Puerto Rico has suffered the compounded effects of multiple disasters since the devastating impacts of hurricanes Irma and Maria in September 2017. At the end of 2019, the island was impacted with recurrent seismic activity in the southwest region, including a magnitude 6.4 earthquake on January 7, 2020. In early 2020, the current COVID-19 pandemic and the resulting health crises induced yet another economic contraction. All these disasters are underscored by a crushing debt crisis and a federally-mandated austerity regime since 2016. Multiple natural disasters have exacerbated vulnerability and poverty; and public energy, telecommunications, water, health, and transportation systems have deteriorated and become even more vulnerable, causing systematic failures in social safety nets.

Recent disasters have revealed serious vulnerabilities in Puerto Rico's preparedness planning, institutional response capacity and coordination, resource management at various levels of implementation, data availability, and the lack of suitable and accessible mechanisms to support adequate local community engagement. As Puerto Rico transitions to long-term recovery, the prospect of one of the largest disaster allocations in Community Development Block Grant funds in U.S. history is increasingly shaping state-level planning and decision-making processes. Used appropriately, these funds represent an opportunity for communities to secure decent housing, adequate infrastructure, and economic recovery.

The collection of studies included in this special volume of *CENTRO Journal* shows evidence of how post-disaster recovery is progressing in Puerto Rico, and the challenges and opportunities for local participation in reconstruction programs. To date, the available evidence leads to a portrait of an uneven recovery, a recovery characterized by the bifurcation of efforts from the civic sector and central and federal governments. Municipalities, the small business community, and nonprofit organizations had active engagement in the initial post disaster emergency phase to the benefit and welfare of victims and communities. For the most part, private and philanthropic donations supported local engagement and disaster relief. The Foundation Center estimates that philanthropic efforts alone raised more than $375 million for relief and recovery from the storms (Red de Fundaciones de Puerto Rico 2019).

In addition to donations from philanthropic organizations but with minimal support from the local or federal government, substantial donations and volunteerism from individuals and the private sector made it possible for the nonprofit sector to have an extensive and impactful participation in the immediate emergency phase of post-disaster recovery (García and Chandrasekhar 2020). In addition to civic sector engagement, federal disaster spending during the emergency phase reached $15 billion—about half of total federal spending for all disasters declared in 2017 in the United States and Puerto Rico. This spending included, for example, the initial rehabilitation of the electrical grid, housing and other assistance to families, and loans and grants to small businesses.

Exacerbating the harshness of the immediate impact of the storms on the island people and economy, a close examination of common indicators stresses that the transition to long-term disaster recovery has been grueling and demanding. Census data for 2018 and 2019 indicate a very modest gain in population, from 3,193,354 in 2018 to 3,193,694 in 2019—an 0.01 percent population increase—

The author (emele@hunter.cuny.edu) is a Professor of Urban Policy and Planning and the Director of the Center for Puerto Rican Studies at Hunter College, CUNY. In addition to numerous scientific papers and other publications, he is the author or editor of thirteen books including *State of Puerto Ricans* (Centro Press, 2017) and *Puerto Ricans at the Dawn of the New Millenium* (Centro Press, 2014), and served as guest editor of *CENTRO Journal*'s "Pathway to Economic Opportunity" (v.23 n.2, 2011) and "Puerto Rico Post-Hurricane Maria: Origins and Consequences of a Crisis" (v.30 n.3, 2018) issues.

definitely within the margin of error for the estimates. Yet the significance of these figures lay in a reversal of more than a decade of steady population decline spurred by a relentless exodus and the signaling of a first step toward recovery. Similarly, a modest increase of 1.6 percent in the Index of Economic Activity (IEA) provides additional evidence of recovery in 2019, barely the second consecutive annual positive growth after five years of uninterrupted declines in the index.

However, because of the economic depression induced by the COVID pandemic, from January to September 2020 the IEA contracted by 5.7 percent. In this context, federal long-term recovery funding allocations to Puerto Rico for disasters declared in 2017 have stalled. From the $19.9 billion congressional allocation to HUD for disaster recovery and mitigation programs for Puerto Rico, as of the end of July 2020, only $96 million had been outlayed. In sum, three years after the 2017 storms that devastated the island, indicators such as economic activity and implementation of recovery programs point toward a stalled long-term recovery.

That said, local capacity for disaster recovery participation is largely a function of the policies and programs that facilitate or hinder civic participation and local engagement.

Local participation and engagement are critical elements for long-term economic recovery (FEMA 2017). The disaster recovery literature has established that community engagement, especially nonprofit and local government participation, is an important determinant of overall community recovery (Dyer 1999; Mileti 1999; Smith and Birkland 2012; Peacock, Morrow and Gladwin 1997; Scott and Murphy 2014; Welsh and Esnard 2009). The nonprofit sector capacity's to participate in the post-disaster economic recovery phase is constrained due to several factors. These factors are related to federal policies that regulate recovery programs and local implementation, and the various stages and capacity requirements for program participation, such as community planning for project development, competing for local and federal funding, and local management of programs. Additionally, there is limited experience in the nonprofit sector with federal housing and economic development, and disaster mitigation programs, which constitute the bulk of the post-disaster economic recovery phase. Even organizations with prior knowledge in community economic development have a limited capacity for real estate development and to meet the Notification of Funding Availability (NOFA) requirements and be competitive for federal disaster recovery and other ancillary funding. That said, local capacity for disaster recovery participation is largely a function of the policies and programs that facilitate or hinder civic participation and local engagement. Such is the dialectic that motivates the studies herein presented.

The studies included in this special volume of *CENTRO Journal* analyze challenges and opportunities for local participation in reconstruction programs and their potential to contribute to post disaster recovery in Puerto Rico. In the next section, I discuss indicators of disaster recovery or lack thereof three years after Hurricanes Irma and Maria ravaged the island. One critical indicator of recovery is business sector responses to the disaster, a topic addressed by Lobato, Álvarez and Aponte (2020) in this volume. Then, I discuss the challenges and opportunities for local participation in long-term recovery. Two studies included in this volume discuss nonprofit sector responses and grassroots innovative initiatives. The García and Chandrasekhar (2020) study focuses on the nonprofit sector response during the emergency recovery phase, and the Villarrubia-Mendoza and Vélez-Vélez (2020) study focuses on the emerging role of grassroots organizations in post-Maria recovery.

The third section of the introduction addresses challenges and opportunities in disaster recovery for the housing and community economic development industry. Meléndez (2020) identifies the absence of specific state-level policies benefiting community development, along with a weak support system, as important factors holding back the nonprofit sector participation in federal economic recovery programs. Borges-Méndez (2020) proposes that there is a disconnection between local implementation of disaster recovery programs, though many organizations already have a proven track record of project completion and are actively overcoming barriers to expand their participation in disaster recovery programs. In the final section of the introduction, Torres Cordero (2020) enumerates more equitable policies from other stateside jurisdictions aimed at producing a better and more just recovery, one that the Government of

Puerto Rico can choose to implement in its CDBG-DR and CDBG-MIT governance.

The last section of the introduction is devoted to highlighting core findings from the studies and policy recommendations. Whether Puerto Rico takes advantage of this unique window of opportunity to restore its economy and infrastructure in a more resilient fashion, while strengthening the nonprofit sector's capacity for community planning, housing development, and neighborhood revitalization remains an open question. The studies included in this volume propose that the long-term benefits of federal disaster recovery programs are contingent on reforming public policy to encourage and support nonprofit developers' participation in developing reconstruction programs, strengthening nonprofit capacity, encouraging partnerships and collaborations, and providing professional development for economic recovery.

Where Is the Recovery Three Years After Hurricanes Irma and Maria?

Common indicators of post-disaster recovery found in the literature include the returning of population to the affected areas after natural disasters, the renewal of business activity, and the successful restoration of damaged infrastructure such as housing, public infrastructure, and government services. In this section I examine empirical indicators associated with these different aspects of disaster recovery.

Climate change and the devastating impact of more frequent and intense natural hazards in the United States and worldwide have induced a renewed effort in understanding post-disaster recovery and building community resilience—the idea that post-disaster reconstruction should go beyond restoring systems to their pre-disaster state and to seek systems' improvements that will mitigate potential damages from future hazard events. A recent review of the literature concluded that despite conceptual and methodological efforts across disciplines, to date we lack a comprehensive community resilience model that incorporates the interdependence of physical infrastructure, social and economic systems (Koliou et al. 2018). In this context, I use the resilience inference measurement (RIM) model to illustrate how different municipalities have adapted to the devastation caused by the 2017 Hurricanes Irma and Maria. The RIM model is adopted to measure community resilience in Puerto Rico because it was successfully used to "quantify resilience to climate-related hazards for 52 U.S. counties along the northern Gulf of Mexico (Lam 2016)," a region that resembles the storms (hazard events) that affected Puerto Rico. The RIM model uses exposure (the relative damage of a hazard event in a municipality), damage (the sum of all damages in a given period of time), and recovery (population change over the period of time) as indicators for the estimation of the index of community resilience. Given these parameters, the RIM model ranks municipalities on four clusters raging from low to high community resilience.

Figure 1 depicts the RIM classification of community resilience between 2016 to 2019, the period prior to and post hazard events, and population change from 2017 to 2019 in Puerto Rico by municipalities. After more than a decade of steady population decline, Puerto Rico experienced a modest one-tenth of one percent (0.01 percent) growth in population in 2019. As a reference point, the island lost more than two percent (-2.39 percent) population in 2017, and almost four percent (-3.97 percent) in 2018, the year immediately after the storms. Evidently the map shows that there is a high correlation between community resilience and municipalities that experienced population decline or modest growth after the storms. The data indicate that municipalities with higher resilience have (to some degree) stalled population losses, while communities with low resilience continue to experience population decline. Municipalities that experienced the highest percentage gains in population and are classified in the high community resilience group include Dorado (1.03 percent population growth), Barceloneta (1.12 percent), Juncos (1.15 percent), Coamo (1.25 percent), Las Piedras (1.30 percent), Naguabo (1.39 percent), Toa Alta (1.39 percent), and Gurabo (2.18 percent). Yet more than half of the municipalities depict low community resilience and a continuation of population loss. In sum, though there are signs of a modest overall recovery as measured by returning population to communities affected by the storms, most communities continue to experience the adverse impact of the disasters and continued population losses.

The loss and renewal of business activity follows a similar pattern to the one observed for post-disaster population losses and returning population across municipalities. Business activity before and after the hurricanes serve as an indicator of recovery. In a study sponsored by the Puerto Rico team of the Global Entrepreneurship Monitor (GEM) longitudinal research project, Lobato, Álvarez and

Figure 1. Community Resilience (2016 to 2019) and Population Change (2017 to 2019) in Puerto Rico.

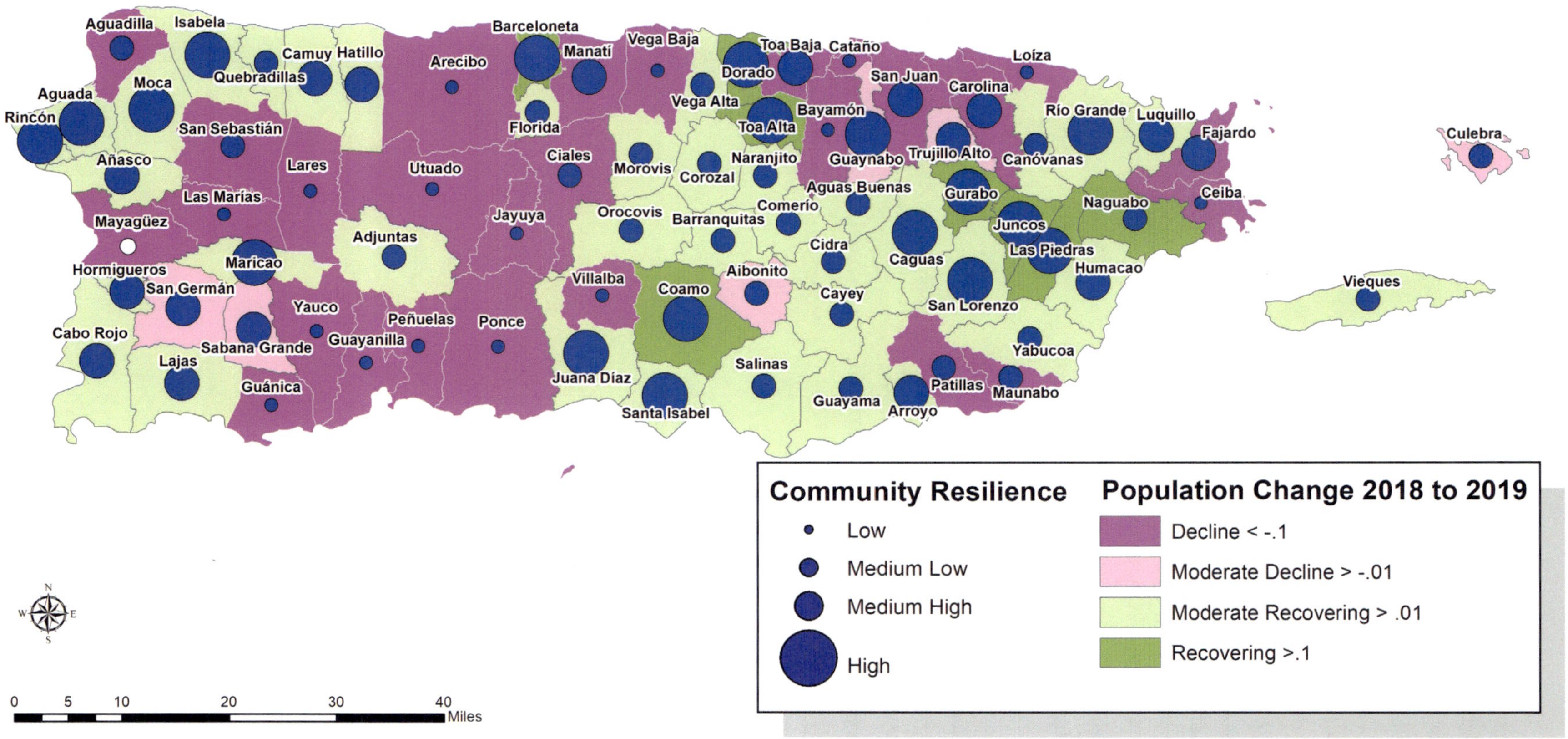

Source: U.S. Bureau of the Census, Puerto Rico Community Survey, Annual estimates, various years. FEMA Housing Assistance dataset.
Notes: Author's estimates and data available upon request.

Aponte show how, immediately after Hurricane Maria, Puerto Rico experienced "unusually high levels of closings of establishments and employment contraction" (2020, 39) But, by the beginning of 2018, from March 2018 to March 2019, business opening jumped 28 percent when compared to the same period the prior year, and the "effect on job creation was even stronger, with a raise of 39 percent in jobs created in newly opened establishments" (Lobato, Álvarez and Aponte 2020, 51). These rates of establishment closings and impact on employment in Puerto Rico are like those in Louisiana after Hurricane Katrina. However, in the case of Puerto Rico, "the rise of opening establishments lasted longer and was accompanied by an increase of expanding establishments from March 2018 on" (2020, 59).

In conclusion, Lobato, Álvarez and Aponte (2020, 62) state that:

> **Despite the fact that Puerto Rico's entrepreneurial activity suffered an initial strong negative effect, it reemerged with strength after the hurricanes. It may seem paradoxical, but the entrepreneurial activity performance observed in Puerto Rico and Louisiana could respond to entrepreneurial resilience behavior exposed in the literature. This hypothesis needs to be tested in future empirical research. Other possible reasons for the increase in business activity could be the injection of aid funds to individuals and businesses. After more than a decade of recession or stagnation, the economy of Puerto Rico is in urgent need of new sources of production and employment, but reports from GEM and other international research projects point out that domestic business activity faces an infertile context; several crucial factors hinder the birth and survival of entrepreneurial initiatives.**

Within this frame of reference, it is important to examine in greater detail the implementation of federal disaster programs for Puerto Rico. FEMA's Public Assistance (PA) Program was deployed immediately after the storms and by the end of July 2020 had outlayed $13.8 billion of the $29.4 allocated, or 46.9 percent of the total (Table 1). Most of the remaining funds are obligated to FEMAs Hazard Mitigation Grant Program (HMGP, Section 404) to help rebuild the electrical grid system ($9.6 billion) and for the recovery of the education system ($2 billion). These new programs are funded under FEMA's Public Assistance Alternative Procedures, pursuant to Section 428 of the Robert T. Stafford Disaster Relief and Emergency Assistance Act. Under these procedures, intended to streamline projects while reducing costs, local jurisdictions could take advantage of a fast track for the approval and processing of small projects of up to $120,000 which may include mitigation projects on undamaged facilities.. In contrast to PA, 404 mitigation projects are considered to be part of the long-term recovery phase. This $3 billion mitigation program is supplemented with $1 billion from the CDBG-DR program to compensate for the local share of the program, for a program total of $4 billion. Though hundreds of submitted projects remain in the agency evaluation stage, in July 2020 FEMA approved "525 letters of intent (LOIs) from municipalities, agencies, and private non-profit organizations in Puerto Rico to be evaluated for risk mitigation" (Correa 2020). These LOIs move to the proposal preparation stage, which may take about a year, and if successful will move to project implementation. Pending LOIs continue the initial evaluation process, and it is expected that, depending on avail-

Table 1. Federal Disaster Spending Data for All Disasters Declared in 2017, United States, and Puerto Rico (Billions)

	Allocated	Obligated	Outlayed
United States (a)	118.6	81.3	42.1
(%)	100%	68.5%	35.5%
DHS-FEMA	49.4	49.4	29.6
HUD	35.4	12.7	0.950
Puerto Rico (b)	56.5	36.7	16.0
(%)	100%	65.0%	28.3%
DHS-FEMA	29.4	29.4	13.8
SBA	2	2	1.3
HUD	19.9	3.2	0.096
CDBG-DR (FA)	1.5	1.5	0.112
CDBG-DR	8.2	1.7	--
CDBG-MIT	8.4	--	--
CDBG-DR (EP)	1.9	--	--
DOD (CE)	2.5	0.095	0.041

Source: FEMA's Spending Explorer, Data as of September 30, 2020.
Notes:
(a) Includes: FEMA and SBA for Harvey, Irma, Maria, 2017, CA Wildfires, and other 2017 Disasters; Harvey, Irma, Maria, 2017, CA Wildfires, and other 2017 Disasters (PL 115-123); Harvey, Irma, Maria, 2017, and CA Wildfires (PL 115-156); Harvey, Irma, Maria, 2017, and CA Wildfires (PL 115-72).
(b) Includes DHS without FEMA and DOC.
(FA) First Allocation February 9, 2018.
(EP) Funding to be allocated specifically for enhancing and improving electrical power infrastructure and systems.
(CE) Corps of Engineers-Civil Works.
Legend:
- Allocated: Congress appropriated the funds;
- Obligated: government has entered a binding agreement to award funding;
- Outlayed: the money has actually been paid.

able funding, additional projects would be invited to move to the proposal preparation stage. Despite extraordinary measures imposed by President Trump's administration to federally funded programs in Puerto Rico (Fadulu and Walker 2020), FEMA's 404 mitigation program is slowly progressing towards implementation.

The situation with Congressional allocations to HUD for disaster recovery and mitigation programs to assist Puerto Rico is more daunting than the implementation of FEMA's long-term mitigation programs. Table 1 depicts federal data for all disasters declared in 2017 in the United States and Puerto Rico.[1] Congress made the first allocation to HUD for CDBG-DR programs for Puerto Rico in February 2018, just a few months after the 2017 hurricanes. The CDBG-DR action plan was initially approved by HUD in February of 2018 and since then has undergone four substantial amendments to date. The initial process of approval of the CDBG-DR action plan for Puerto Rico conforms to the timetable for other jurisdictions. Yet, the CDGB-MIT program, which with a $8.4 billion is the largest allocation for HUD programs for disaster mitigation in Puerto Rico, just completed the public comments phase of the action plan and is currently undergoing revisions for final approval.

HUD's disaster programs implementation in Puerto Rico lags in comparison to other jurisdictions. Of the initial allocation of $1.5 billion in February 2018, disbursed primarily for housing rehabilitation and assistance, only $96 million had been outlayed as of the end of July 2020. In a similar fashion, to date only $3.2 billion of the $19.9 billion has been obligated to program projects or administrative expenses. According to Martin (2018), the typical process "take 9–12 months after an Action Plan is approved (which typically occurs within months of HUD allocation notice) to hire staff, procure contractors and consultants, and develop management and information systems." By this standard, which is based on an examination of CDBG-DR grantees action plans for disasters from 2003 to 2014, so far program implementation in Puerto Rico is taking twice longer than the typical timeline for other jurisdictions across the United States. Based on the cumulative evidence from stateside jurisdictions, Martin asserts that in regard to typical disaster projects, "[w]ithin the same sample of grants, housing activities on average take 4.7 years to complete from the time a disaster is declared, and overall grants (including non-housing activities) on average take 5.1 years" (2018, 5). Considering CDBG-DR program implementation to date, we should expect Puerto Rico's program completion to exceed the typical CDBG-DR program implementation timeline elsewhere.

Housing rehabilitation, reconstruction, or facilitating relocation of disaster victims in Puerto Rico are activities tailor made for CDCs.

To date, the Puerto Rico Department of Housing CDBG-DR contracts totaling $723 million have gone entirely to the private sector, with 62 percent of this total awarded to foreign corporations (Meléndez 2020, 130, Table 3). These contracts are primarily for the Repair, Reconstruction, or Relocation (R3) housing program, which represents 24 percent of the total allocation of $3 billion to this program. Though the nonprofit sector capacity to bid for these contracts was restricted given the specifications of the Notification of Funding Availability (NOFA) of the Puerto Rico Department of Housing (PRDOH) as approved by HUD, other stateside jurisdictions have implemented more inclusive policies to support capacity building for municipalities and local nonprofit contractors. Housing rehabilitation, reconstruction, or facilitating relocation of disaster victims in Puerto Rico are activities tailor made for CDCs. Many of the CDCs are already implementing some of these activities in a modest scale with support from the private sector. Given the appropriate policy (i.e., a more inclusive NOFA), CDCs are positioned to participate as contractors in future allocations of the remaining three-quarters of funds in this program.

PRDOH's CDBG-DR program subrecipients agreements have earmarked Government of Puerto Rico agencies, municipalities, and nonprofit organizations. Of the total $679 million of PRDOH's agreements with CDBG-DR subrecipients from 2018 to 2020, 84 percent was allocated to government agencies and two newly created government-affiliated nonprofit organizations. Municipalities are earmarked to receive 5.5 percent, and nonprofits were allocated 12.7 percent (Meléndez 2020, 131, Table 4). Considering both contracts and agreements totaling $1.4 billion, $723 million (or 52 percent) are allocated to the private sector (of which two-thirds are assigned to foreign corporations), central government agencies are earmarked to receive $556 million (40 percent), non-government-affiliated nonprofit organizations are earmarked to receive $86 million (6 percent), and municipalities $38 million (2.7 percent). Despite the grim picture of CDBG-DR allocations supporting program activities implemented by nonprofit organizations and municipalities, it is important to consider that the CDBG-DR programs implementation is in its initial phases, and the CDBG-MIT action plan is still in the approval stage. A change in administrations in local government and stateside could lead to a policy framework more inclusive of nonprofit organizations and municipalities, and the bulk of federal disaster funding remains to be allocated.

In sum, three years after the Major Disaster Declaration by federal authorities in relation to the 2017 hurricanes in Puerto Rico, economic, population, and disaster program indicators offer a picture of an uneven and sluggish recovery. For one, despite the lack of coordination and erratic response from the federal and Puerto Rico governments to the catastrophic event and the collapse of the public infrastructure, the nonprofit sector, with support from the philanthropic and private sectors and local businesses, had a strong initial response during the emergency phase of recovery. But the transition to long-term recovery, which requires implementation of disaster recovery programs, has been sluggish and largely divorced from engagement of local resources. The next section examines the nonprofit sector in Puerto Rico and its ongoing and potential participation in economic recovery.

The Nonprofit Sector in Puerto Rico and Its Participation in Economic Recovery

The catalyst role of nonprofit organizations in mobilizing local resources, coordinating emergency services with government, and advocating for more resilient community infrastructure is well established in the literature (Eller et al. 2015; Luna 2013; Patterson et al. 2010; Robinson and Murphy 2014). However, one of the critical questions for disaster recovery policy in Puerto Rico is whether local nonprofit organizations are capable to implement programs effectively. This question is partially related to the sector's capacity in general, and specifically to its experience and ability to participate in federal recovery programs over a long period. I begin this section providing an overall portrait of the nonprofit sector in Puerto Rico, and then summarizing key findings from the García and Chandrasekhar (2020) study on the nonprofit sector response during the emergency recovery phase and the Villarrubia-Mendoza and Vélez-Vélez (2020) study on the emerging role of grassroots organizations in post-Maria recovery.

Table 2. Employment in Puerto Rico by Sector, 2019 (Civilian population aged 16 years and older)

Private	661,320	70.9%
Self-employed	26,671	2.9%
Nonprofit	40,676	4.4%
Government	204,510	21.9%
Total	933,177	100.0%

Source: U.S. Census Bureau, 2019 1-year American Community Survey, TableID: C24060.

First, as depicted in Table 2, the nonprofit sector in Puerto Rico employs 40,676 (or 4.4 percent) of the civilian population aged 16 and older. To put in context, the nonprofit sector constitutes 10 percent of the American workforce In short, though the nonprofit sector constitutes a significant portion of the Puerto Rico economy and workforce, it is about half the size of this sector for the average state.

Figure 2 illustrates the various types of non-governmental organizations (NGOs) comprising the nonprofit universe. Keeping in mind that the graphic is intended to illustrate a concept and not actual proportions of industry share, all nonprofit organizations are NGOs. We use this distinction to denote a significant group of international charitable organizations known typically as NGOs. This type of organization is active in the United States and includes well- recognized organizations such as the International Olympic Committee and Amnesty International among many others. Conversely, there are U.S.-based NGOs with hefty international portfolios such as the Red Cross or the Salvation Army. The legal definition of a nonprofit in the United States is that they are charitable IRS Exempt Organizations.

For analytical purposes, as illustrated in Figure 2, I divide the nonprofit sector engaged in community development into two types of organizations: community-based organizations (CBOs) and community development corporations (CDCs). Both organization types are place-based, which distinguishes them from other nonprofit organizations. CBOs and CDCs have a focus on one or several neighborhoods, and they may operate at a local, regional, or national level. CDCs are the backbone of the community development industry. Many CDCs include social services, community planning and organizing, and programs typical

Figure 2. Types of Non-Governmental Organizations

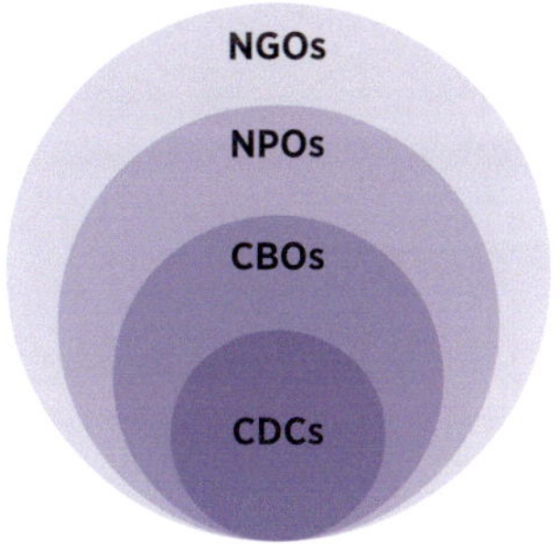

of other types of CBOs or nonprofit organizations, yet they are distinct from other community organizations because they focus on affordable housing, business development and other revenue-generating economic development projects (Meléndez and Servon 2007).

The nonprofit sector in Puerto Rico comprises 1,510 organizations registered with the Puerto Rico State Department and 114 cooperatives registered with the Corporación Pública para Supervisión y Seguro de Cooperativas de Puerto Rico (COSSEC). Of these 1,608 organizations, 466 were IRS exempt organizations. In 2019, as depicted in Table 3, the 466 IRS exempt organizations in Puerto Rico that filed 990 returns (for calendar year 2018), arguably the more robust cohort within the nonprofit sector in Puerto Rico, reported $3 billion in total revenues and $7 billion in assets. Whether measured by average revenues or assets, health and education organizations represent the bulk of large nonprofit organizations. These sectors include the top hospitals and universities in the island, some of them exceeding annual revenues and assets of over one hundred million. The cooperative sector also includes large organizations. It is necessary to keep in mind that less than one-third of all the cooperatives filed 990 returns as IRS exempt organizations and therefore the average revenues and assets are not representative of the industry as a whole. According to the most recent financial filings submitted to the COSSEC in 2018, there were 114 cooperatives in Puerto Rico with $8.8 billion in assets, 996,132 members, and 2,899 employees (COSSEC 2018). A handful of credit unions are also CDFIs. Though the participation of coops in the affordable housing development industry is limited, a significant number of coops provide housing mortgages to their members.

However, whether nonprofit organizations can successfully navigate the dynamism and uncertainty of the disaster recovery process in Puerto Rico remains an open question. Research shows that networking and communication can provide community organizations with new avenues of information and action (Quarantelli 1999), boost their diminished capacities, provide better means of community representation, and improve "cognition" of "emerging risk to which a community is exposed and to act on that information" (Comfort 2007). Evidence also suggests that neighborhoods that undertake social networking may be better able to respond to disasters because it facilitates information exchange, collective action, and access to new resources for recovery (Aldrich 2012). Community organizations play a critical role in disaster recovery, given their ability to motivate volunteerism, assess local needs, and distribute goods and aid (Patterson et al. 2010).

Table 3. IRS-Exempt Organization Returns Filed in Calendar Year 2019 (From 990 Forms)

		REVENUE		ASSETS	
Sector	**Count**	**Total**	**Average**	**Total**	**Average**
Arts, Culture, and Humanities	23	29,126,795	1,266,382	85,557,722	3,719,901
Cooperatives	16	141,527,602	8,845,475	2,525,222,028	157,826,377
Education	89	1,014,567,503	11,399,635	1,829,698,789	20,558,413
Health	81	1,378,082,922	17,013,369	1,495,944,636	18,468,452
Housing and Com. Devel.	58	46,655,404	804,404	173,006,470	2,982,870
Comm, Dev. Corp. (CDCs)	12	12,124,396	1,010,366	56,257,777	4,688,148
Human Services	117	176,099,476	1,505,124	200,975,876	1,717,743
Other Civic	53	167,839,988	3,166,792	158,677,918	2,993,923
Public Safety	29	76,149,905	2,625,859	514,656,348	17,746,771
TOTAL	466	3,030,049,595	6,476,234	6,983,739,787	50,566

Sources: https://www.irs.gov/statistics/soi-tax-stats-annual-extract-of-tax-exempt-organization-financial-data; and https://www.irs.gov/charities-non-profits/exempt-organizations-business-master-file-extract-eo-bmf/.

Figure 3. Objectives of Work Focus or Social Impact of Nonprofits in Puerto Rico

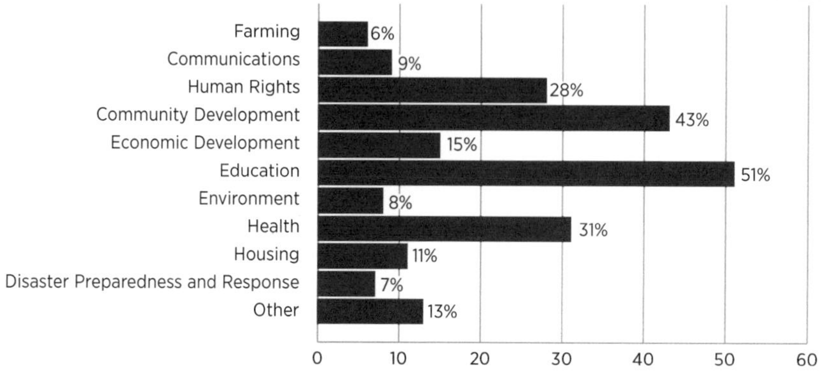

Source: García and Chandrasekhar (2020). Impact of Hurricane Maria to the civic sector and disaster recovery capacity in Puerto Rico Survey, 2019. Center for Puerto Rican Studies, Hunter College CUNY.

With support from the Center for Puerto Rican Studies, García and Chandrasekhar (2020) conducted a study to ascertain the role of nonprofits in disaster recovery, organizational and networking capacity, and to what extent they are implementing capacity-building measures. Selecting randomly from the universe of nonprofit organizations in Puerto Rico, they completed 235 telephone interviews as well as in-depth interviews with twenty-one residents and executive directors of agencies.

First, the survey requested organizations to identify the most frequent challenges that were faced since the hurricane. As depicted in Table 4 and might be expected, respondents reported the most frequent challenge faced since the hurricane were damages to their building infrastructure and facilities (45 percent). The second most frequent response was an increase in demand for services provided by the organization (14 percent). "Other" refers to loss of funding, lack of information on grants, greater bureaucracy, and lack of communication, among other answers. In terms of existing capacity, they found that the primary focus of organizations were education programs, with community development and health the next most prominent (Figure 3). Yet, it is noticeable that housing and economic development, the core activities of CDCs and the focus of reconstruction programs, were activities reported by a relatively small number of organizations, 20 percent or less of organizations.

Significant findings from the García and Chandrasekhar (2020) study are as follows:

1. the natural disaster had a significant impact in non-profit organizations physically and operationally, while interactions with other local nonprofits have increased substantially. But nonprofits organizations feel less connected to the government;
2. there is a lot of energy in the non-profit sector, as demonstrated by increased demand for services and changing missions to respond to this demand;
3. there has been intensified local interaction among non-profits; however, non-profits are not "hooked" into formal recovery structures (funding or information) mainly relating to government, and it is somewhat of a surprise that disaster preparedness is not among the top choices for programmatic development; and
4. organizations want more help with capacity building across the board—from better understanding of recovery programs to grant-writing—to close a large gap between availability of funding and successful acquisition of grants.

The García and Chandrasekhar (2020) study indicates that local nonprofit organizations are deeply embedded in communities and should be encouraged to participate in recovery efforts. Yet findings from the survey of nonprofit organizations in Puerto Rico indicate the urgent need to improve the capacity of local community organizations to participate more effectively in disaster recovery. There is a lack of organizations dedicated to or with the capacity to implement housing and economic development—which are key competencies required for local and federal recovery programs. Effective participation from nonprofit organizations

Table 4. Nonprofit Organizational Challenges in Puerto Rico Post-Maria

Category	Number	Percent
Affected buildings	105	45%
Loss of employees	16	7%
Loss of information or data	15	6%
More demand for services	34	14%
Lack of knowledge regarding reconstruction	9	4%
Other	55	24%
Total	234	100%

Source: García and Chandrasekhar (2020). Impact of Hurricane Maria to the civic sector and disaster recovery capacity in Puerto Rico Survey, 2019. Center for Puerto Rican Studies, Hunter College CUNY.

would require access to government and federal recovery funding for community projects. In part, there is a great need for more inclusive policies that support local capacity building for reconstruction, and in part the allocation of funding needs to be more independent from the local political structure. According to responses to the survey, to date nonprofits participating in economic recovery are mostly being funded by private sources and members' contributions. Although nonprofit organizations might have knowledge about federal funding opportunities, they are not applying successfully for this funding or, when they apply, are not being successful in accessing these funds. Beside the need to have policies that encourage participation, these findings indicate that there is a clear need for technical assistance and capacity building for accessing federal funding. These findings from the survey are a first step torward an understanding of how nonprofit organizations have an interest and are eager to increase their capacity to engage in disaster recovery.

The Villarrubia-Mendoza and Vélez-Vélez (2020) study on the emerging role of grassroots organizations in Post-Maria recovery, included as part of this volume of *CENTRO Journal,* examines citizens grassroot participation and local engagement in disaster recovery in Puerto Rico through the prism of the emergence of community-based initiatives known as "centros de apoyo mutuo" (mutual support centers) or CAMs across the island. CAMs are projects based on principles of *"autogestión"* and are associated in the disaster recovery literature as grassroots community organizing, mutual aid (*"ayuda mutua," "apoyo mutuo"*), community empowerment and economic development, and social movements associated with resistance to top-down state initiatives.[7] The study involved over a year of ethnographic participant observation and conducted in-depth interviews with leaders and members of nine of the CAMs that emerged after the 2017 hurricanes. According to the Villarrubia-Mendoza and Vélez-Vélez (2020) study, CAMs engage in a wide range of projects and initiatives including community-coop housing programs, energy independence, sustainable agriculture, and entrepreneurship capacitation, among others. Through community engagement these organizations are redefining a vision of a more inclusive recovery process that encompasses a broader social transformation. They are confronting and raising awareness about pro-forma participation in CDBG funding hearings, denial of access to ownership deeds of abandoned schools and buildings, or the continued undermining of the basic needs of impacted communities.

Three years after Hurricane Maria devastated Puerto Rico, CAMs continue providing a grassroot model for reconstruction and community resilience, a model of a recovery process that questions how institutional structures have distributed the manifestation of damage. CAMs establish a framework that seek to improve socio-economic conditions within their communities, producing a model for social transformation beyond the disaster context. As these grassroot groups engage in social entrepreneurship they are confronted with the challenges that nonprofit organizations in general confront—how to sustain these alternative models of recovery while continuing to challenge the current disaster recovery process and reconstruction programs. In the next section of this article I examine how nonprofit organizations and community development corporations (CDCs)—organizations that specialize in housing and community economic development—build capacity to be able to take advantage of the window of opportunity provided by the reconstruction process and disaster recovery

The Housing and Community Economic Development Industry and the Economic Recovery of Puerto Rico

There is a unique window of opportunity in Puerto Rico to capitalize on federal reconstruction funding to support the development of a more robust housing and community development industry, anchored on principles of social entrepreneurship as a foundation for neighborhood revitalization and local economic development. Social enterprises[8] and ventures are undertakings by private, nonprofit organizations or special units of local government that operate as businesses. Yet social enterprise, a core component of the stateside community development industry, which is also arguably the foundation of the most developed subsectors among nonprofits in Puerto Rico (e.g., cooperatives, education and health), is a critical need among community development and human services nonprofits in Puerto Rico, especially considering the critical role that the community development industry could play in economic reconstruction. There are numerous reasons for the existing capacity or lack thereof of the community development industry and the use of federal funding for the development of social projects in Puerto Rico. As I will discuss below, the absence of specific state-level policies benefiting and often impeding development, along with a weak support system, are important factors holding back the nonprofit sector participation in federal economic recovery programs.

The distinction between community-based organizations (CBOs) and community development corporations (CDCs) is particularly relevant in the context of implementing federally funded recovery programs. Though both types of nonprofit organization are place-based, CDCs specialize in housing rehabilitation, affordable housing development, business development, and other revenue generating economic development projects (Meléndez and Servon 2007). These organizational capacities are necessary for most disaster recovery projects. Table 5 shows the CDBG-DR programs for Puerto Rico totaling $9 billion. Of this total, 50 percent of funding is devoted to housing, 15 percent to economic development, 14 percent to city (neighborhood) revitalization, and 1.2 percent to community planning. Besides having been incorporated under IRS Section 501(c)(3), affordable housing rehabilitation and construction program participation requires nonprofit organizations to be certified by the Department of Housing and Urban Development (HUD) as Community Housing Development Organization (CHDO), or to be certified as a Local Housing Counseling Agency (LHCA) to assist consumers to participate in HUD and other federal agencies housing subsidies programs. CDCs often obtain additional certifications from the U.S. Department of Treasury as a Community Development Financial Institution (CDFI) or a Community Development Entity (CDE). These certifications are a precondition for receiving federal funding for certain community development programs.[9] CBOs lacking these capacities face either a sudden capacity building challenge, or the need to partner with CDCs that possess these capacities and certifications to participate in federally funded reconstruction programs.

The relative size and strength of the housing and community development industry in Puerto Rico must be understood in the context of the nonprofit and cooperatives sectors. Assessing the housing and community development nonprofit subsector by the same metrics we used before, this subsector has the lowest averages for revenues and assets, except for the human services subsector (Table 3). If we consider the nonprofit sector to be inclusive of all the cooperatives, whether these are IRS exempt organizations or not, the total asset base of this sector as a whole in 2018 adds to over $13 billion in assets, of which the housing and community development sector and the CDC subsector represent a very small fraction. We have identified one dozen active CDCs, including some (currently or formerly) CHDOs, and about half a dozen CDFIs in Puerto Rico. In reference to Table 3, the CDCs in Puerto Rico rank as the organizations with the lowest average assets, and the second lowest average revenues. According to Borges-Méndez (2020), CDCs exhibit a wide range of capacity to implement development projects, most have limited capacity for housing and real estate development, and only few have undertaken any recovery-related projects other than housing rehabilitation and other emergency-related activities. As in the case of the community development industry in the United States, housing policy has had a determinant influence on the history of housing and community development in Puerto Rico, and it is perhaps the most significant element shaping the trajectory of the local industry.

Table 5. CDBG-DR Programs (Millions)

PROGRAM	ASSIGNMENT	PERCENTAGE
Planning	150	1.7%
Puerto Rico Geospatial Framework (GeoFrame) Program	50	
Municipal Recovery Planning Program	39	
Whole Community Resilience Planning Program	55	
Home Resilience Innovation Competition Program	6	
Housing	4,489	50.1%
Home Repair, Reconstruction, or Relocation Program	3,026	
Rental Assistance Program	10	
Homebuyer Assistance Program	350	
Title Clearance Program	40	
Social Interest Housing Program	33	
CDBG-DR Gap to Low Income Housing Tax Credits Program (LIHTC)	413	
Housing Counseling Program	18	
Community Energy and Water Resilience Installations Program	300	
Multi-family Reconstruction, Repair, and Resilience Program	300	
Economy	1,318	14.7%
Re-grow PR Urban-Rural Agriculture Program	93	
Small Business Incubators and Accelerators Program	35	
Small Business Financing Program	225	
Workforce Training Program	40	
Construction and Commercial Revolving Loan Program	100	
Economic Development Investment Portfolio for Growth Program	800	
Tourism & Business Marketing Program	25	
Infrastructure	1,475	16.5%
Non-Federal Match Program	1,000	
Community Resilience Centers Program	75	
Critical Infrastructure Resilience Program	400	
Multi-Sector	1,523	17.0%
City Revitalization Program	1,223	
Puerto Rico by Design Program	300	
Total	8,954	100%

Source: Puerto Rico Department of Housing, CDBG-DR Program. Accessed 10-6-20 from: https://cdbg-dr.pr.gov/en/.

In 2009 and 2010, nonprofit developers built more affordable housing using federal tax credits than private developers who up to that point (and after the ARRA program ended) dominated the industry.

In a study included in this special issue of *CENTRO Journal* and sponsored by the Center for Puerto Rican Studies, I identified three significant barriers that have hindered the development of the community economic development industry in Puerto Rico: the exclusionary role of federal and local recovery funding policy; the relative weakness of the industry ecosystem; and the relative scarcity of professionals with community development skills, especially professionals with the understanding of reconstruction programs (Meléndez 2020). The potential role that CDCs can play in the implementation of disaster recovery programs is illustrated by a case study of the impact of nonprofit developers in affordable housing construction after the American Recovery and Reinvestment Act (ARRA) of 2009 was enacted. In 2009 and 2010,

Programa de Educación Continua para la Recuperación de Puerto Rico Posdesastre

Continuing Education Program for Puerto Rico's Post Disaster Recovery

Programa De Educacion Continua

Email Facebook Twitter LinkedIn

Este programa ofrece capacitación a profesionales involucrados en la recuperación económica de Puerto Rico tras los desastres que ha sufrido. El programa ofrece una serie de cursos a modo de educación continua en base a destrezas de capacitación para que los profesionales de la recuperación económica adquieran las destrezas necesarias para enfrentar un contexto nuevo y desafiante: el impacto cumulativo de la pandemia de COVID-19, la crisis económica, el azote del huracán María y los terremotos, y la manera de aprovechar las oportunidades que ofrecen los fondos federales CDBG-DR y de mitigación, entre otros.

En este contexto, uno de los obstáculos fundamentales para fomentar la participación comunitaria y la participación del sector sin fines de lucro en la recuperación económica es el número insuficiente de profesionales con las habilidades y la experiencia para implementar proyectos de vivienda y de desarrollo económico; y para los municipios, la falta de profesionales que dirijan proyectos de planificación económica. Una evaluación de las tareas y competencias asociadas con la recuperación económica y la planificación comunitaria apunta a la necesidad de hacer disponible la capacitación profesional interdisciplinaria que faculte a los participantes a recopilar y analizar datos relevantes para la implementación de proyectos de recuperación, y que fomente la comprensión de las regiones, la reconstrucción municipal y el contexto de política pública posdesastre en el que operan estos programas.

Los cursos del programa se ajustan a los conjuntos de aptitudes específicas para la contratación de servicios profesionales en las convocatorias emitidas por el Departamento de Vivienda de Puerto Rico (DVPR) para los programas financiados por CDBG-DR, CDBG-MIT; FEMA; la Oficina Central de Recuperación, Reconstrucción y Resiliencia (COR3); y otras agencias federales (e.g., USDA, SBA, EDA) y estatales a cargo de la reconstrucción económica y la mitigación. La certificación de competencia que ofreceremos parte de la premisa de que tanto los funcionarios de estas agencias como los contratistas responsables de implementar estos programas requieren un conocimiento básico que ya tienen otros funcionarios de agencias estatales y municipales, organizaciones sin fines de lucro, negocios y otros colaboradores esenciales para que estos programas se lleven a cabo exitosamente. La adquisición de destrezas necesarias para la recuperación económica es fundamental para los empleados existentes o para el personal que estos colaboradores (patronos municipales o sin fines de lucro) contratarán para el desarrollo y la ejecución de proyectos para la recuperación económica posdesastre.

Los primeros tres cursos del programa son de fundamentos o de introducción. La certificación requiere completar dos de estos tres cursos básicos, además de tres cursos electivos, y la práctica: el curso "Redacción de propuestas exitosas". La práctica se centra en el desarrollo de una propuesta de proyecto de desarrollo económico, que incluye financiamiento y presupuesto, para una organización comunitaria o un municipio.

REGISTRO

Centro PRs Post Disaster Recovery Co...

Post Disaster Recovery Courses and Certification

Centro HUNTER

Interdisciplinario

Planificación · Política pública · Economía

METAS Y OBJETIVOS

Instructores / Instructors

CURSOS

Mitigación y marco de recuperación ante desastres

"Nuevos cursos"
"New courses coming soon"

Conceptos y métodos para la reconstrucción económica

Planificación para la recuperación posdesastre

Fondos CDBG-DR y otros fondos de recuperación económica

La vivienda en recuperación económica y revitalización urbana

Modelos, sostenibilidad y opciones legales para la empresa social

Administración y manejo de subvenciones federales

Financiación y desarrollo de viviendas y edificios comerciales

Desarrollo de la producción agrícola y agronegocios

Cómo comenzar o transformar una organización sin fines de lucro (OSFL) en una corporación de desarrollo comunitario (CDC)

Cómo desarrollar un centro comunal resiliente y de desarrollo económico y social

PRACTICA

Redacción de propuestas exitosas

REGISTRO

Certificación Profesional de Recuperación Posdesastre
Centro de Estudios Puertorriqueños
(Hunter College/CUNY)

Booklets

Puerto Rico Post-Hurricane
Few Americans will forget the controversy over President Donald Trump's...

State of Puerto Ricans 2017
THE STATE OF PUERTO RICANS 2017 Edited by Edwin Meléndez and Carlos Vargas...

Puerto Rico in Crisis
Since 2006 Puerto Rico has been facing an unprecedented economic and...

U.S. Citizenship in Puerto

Biografías de Instructores

Instructors' bios

Descripción de los cursos

Course descriptions

Conozca los cursos obligatorios y optativos

Learn about required and elective courses

Registro

Register

Leer más sobre la certificación

Read more about certification

Ver video introductorio

Watch introductory video

Ir a / Go to:
https://centropr.hunter.cuny.edu/education/ec

RebuildPR Web Map Application

Aplicación de mapa web RebuildPR

Design your map: base map, key info, summary, print

Diseñe su mapa: mapa base, información clave, resumen e imprima

Select layer

Seleccionar capa del tablero

Share your map when completed

Comparta su mapa cuando esté completo

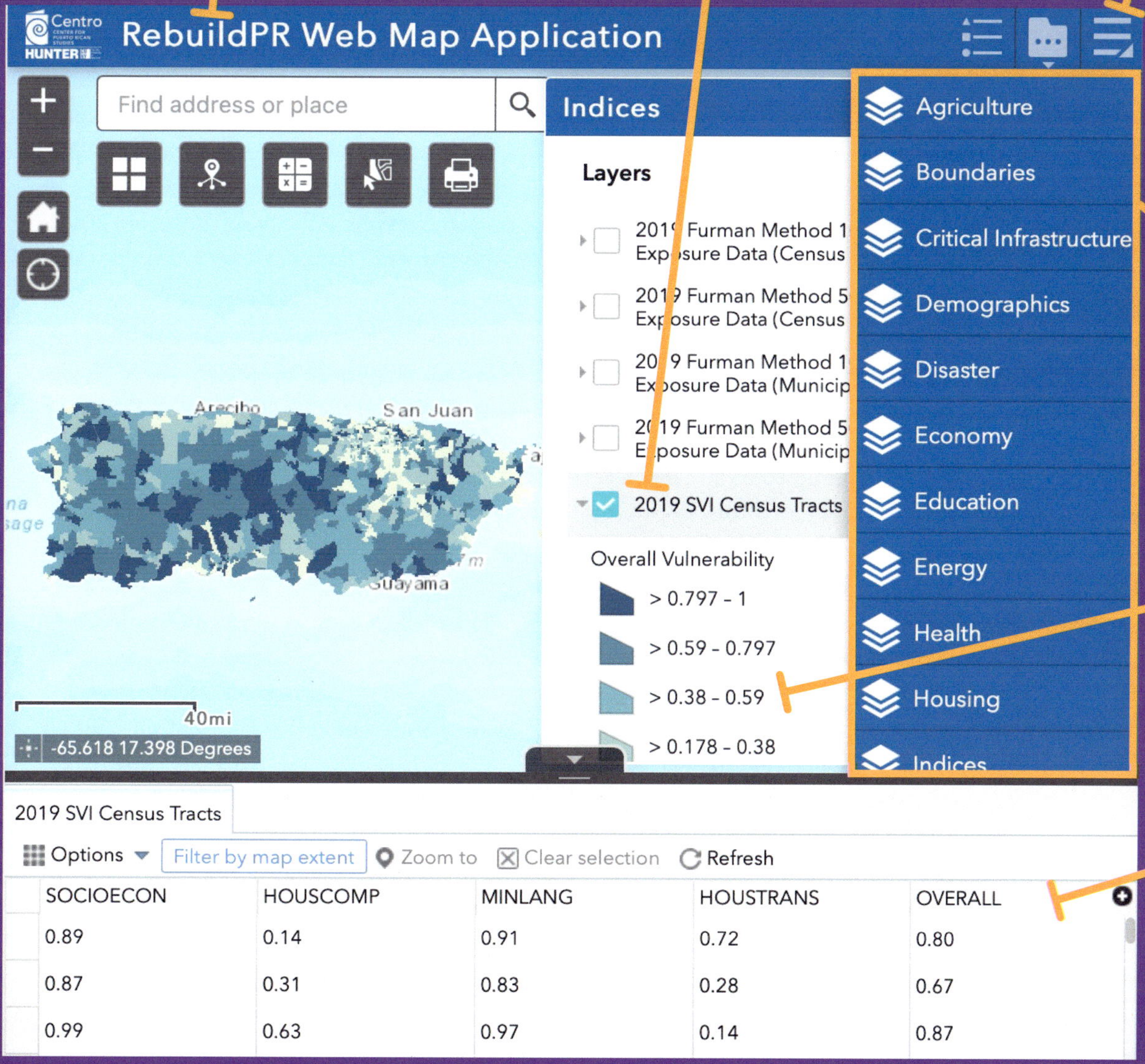

Thematic layers

Panel de control de capas temáticas

Legend

Leyenda

Display layer data as a table

Mostrar datos de capa como una tabla

Ir a / Go to:
https://centropr.hunter.cuny.edu/rebuildpr-web-map-application

Figure 4. Community Economic Development Ecosystem

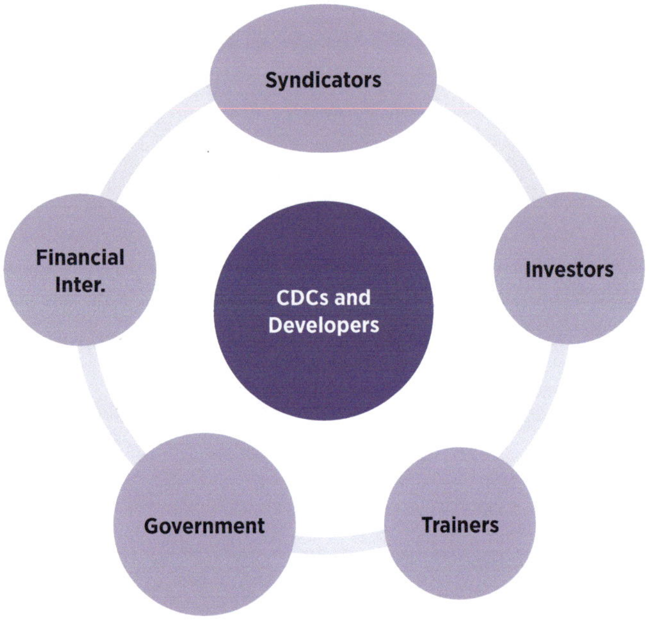

nonprofit developers built more affordable housing using federal tax credits than private developers who up to that point (and after the ARRA program ended) dominated the industry. During the four-year window provided by the ARRA funding, nonprofit developers built over 3,000 units of housing. This is a particularly important finding in the current context of post-disaster economic recovery and the use of CDBG-DR funding for housing rehabilitation, reconstruction, and new construction. Given an inclusive policy implementation, nonprofit developers were able to quickly respond to the challenge and developed as many units as the private sector, demonstrating a rapid deployment capability and surpassing private sector production in the initial years of the program (Meléndez 2020).

As illustrated in Figure 4, the community economic development ecosystem is integrated by CDCs, CDFIs and other financial intermediaries (such as capacity building and training vendors, often subsidiaries or affiliated with financial intermediaries), and other sector-specific networks that play a key role as regional and national advocacy coalitions for the advancement of the industry. Besides disaster mitigation and recovery funding, community economic development is financed through multiple federal programs, and often these programs are combined to finance different aspects of a project. programs broadly utilized in the industry include the LIHTC and HOME for subsidization of affordable housing, CDFIs for low interest community lending, New Market Tax Credits (NMTC) for commercial development, USDA programs for housing and other rural development, EDA programs for local economic development programs, SBA small business support programs, and many others. These federal programs are often paired with state and local subsidies. Yet, in Puerto Rico, many federal social purpose programs are grossly underutilized. The current window of opportunity for the island is given by the availability of reconstruction funding and of other underutilized non-disaster related federal programs. In Louisiana after Hurricane Katrina, for example, LIHTC 4-percent funding was combined with CDBG-DR for leveraging $1.1 billion for the development of 8,448 units, of which 63 percent were affordable (Severino 2018). In Puerto Rico, the current CDBG-DR program allocates $413 million to the LIHTHC-Gap program to provide gap funding for financing affordable rental housing units.

Puerto Rico has a relatively weak community economic development ecosystem. With the notable exception of Banco Popular, which holds a portfolio of affordable housing investments, the island has no significant community economic development financial intermediaries. However, disaster recovery programs offer an opportunity for emerging intermediaries to expand their portfolios. There are two nonprofit organizations that were created to serve as community development intermediaries with programs to support nonprofit and private organizations. Founded in 1984, the Puerto Rico Community Foundation (PRCF) is perhaps the oldest organization with an established program to support organizations' community-based economic development and social entrepreneurship, and to a far less extent, affordable housing. Founded in 2011, Foundation for Puerto Rico (FPR) is a nonprofit organization implementing an economic development initiative based on destination tourism in partnership with local governments and nonprofits organizations. Beginning in 2019, FPR received $37.5 million CDBG-DR funding from the Puerto Rico Department of Housing to lead the coordination of the Whole Community Resilience Planning Program (Foundation for Puerto Rico 2019). According to the Foundation Center, in 2019, FPR and PRCF received $6 million in grants to support community organizations (Meléndez 2020, 143, Table 6).

Beside the FCPR and the FPR, there are two other important organizations that are initiating or renewing efforts for community development programs and potentially can have great impact on fostering social entrepreneurship in Puerto Rico. Two of the most important emerging community development intermediaries are established as public trusts. The Puerto Rico Science, Technology & Research Trust (PRTRT) has undertaken several social ventures and developed specific business development models that serve as capacity-building and financial intermediaries especially for technology companies. The PRDOH recently allocated $92.5 million from the CDBG-DR program to the PRTRT for the implementation of the Re-grow PR Urban-Rural Agriculture Program. Para la Naturaleza (PLN) is a nonprofit subsidiary of the Conservation Trust of Puerto Rico that oversees 42 natural areas throughout the island that are managed as social ventures, and implement fundraising, educational and volunteerism initiatives. These two public trusts have played a prominent role in reconstruction, implemented numerous programs with local community organizations, and have the revenues and assets capacity to evolve into anchors of the community development industry. Despite having a robust cooperative sector, evident gaps in the emergent community economic development industry eco-system are a specialized intermediary supporting and financing affordable housing development, and a high-risk pre-development fund.

The development of CDCs and by implication the housing and community development industry in Puerto Rico is in part a workforce development challenge (Meléndez 2020). In Puerto Rico, there is a wealth and abundant supply of well-trained, talented, and experienced nonprofit and business professionals but not enough professionals with the understanding of reconstruction programs and other federal programs supporting the housing and community development industry. A survey of professionals directly involved or overseeing programs that are part of or align with the economic and disaster recovery plans for Puerto Rico sponsored by the Center for Puerto Rican Studies documented a significant skills gap in critical areas such as community engagement and planning, economic and housing development, and disaster preparedness, recovery and resilience. Even among those most educated and actively engaged in the industry there is a recognition for the need for the development of professional skills in the industry moving forward (Meléndez 2020).

Too few CDCs with significant operational capacity are a tangible barrier to the potential expansion of financial intermediaries, the community economic development industry, and more specifically to the nonprofit sector participation in federally funded disaster recovery programs. CDCs typically maintain a steady pipeline of local development projects or the volume required for syndication and reasonable returns on the investment of financial intermediaries' organizational resources. In a study included in this volume and sponsored by the Center for Puerto Rican Studies, Borges-Méndez (2020) examines the organizational capacity and potential for participation in disaster recovery programs. Among the CDCs selected for the study, some were certified as CHDOs and CDFIs, but they operated other programs such as vocational education, special education, housing counseling, and others. This mix of education and social service, typical of CBOs, is related to the CDC's origins and mission. Many of them were created as CBOs and evolved into CDCs, while a smaller fraction were founded specifically for community economic development activities.

According to Borges-Méndez (2020), CDCs' experience with federal funding is limited and uneven. Though these CDCs have managed HUD (e.g., HOME, LIHTC) and FEMA (Public Assistance) contracts, they reported a limited capacity to prepare complex, multi-year projects, such as those of the CBDG-DR. Among the barriers for disaster recovery program participation they reported the following:

- The complexity of federal funding applications and the short project development cycle imposed by federal agencies;
- The limited project management and compliance expertise of the staff since every funding stream comes with its own reporting requirements;
- Limited outreach resources and methodologies to involve communities and other potential stakeholders in strategic planning, a salient requirement of federal applications.

In addition, CDC leaders were particularly critical of an opportunistic environment in the search for local and federal funding at the municipal level and would like disaster recovery programs to have greater autonomy from the island's political system and electoral cycle. Participating organizations recognized the imperative need to build organizational capacity in general and specifically for disaster programs participation but identified lack of funding and the "downtime" of senior staff while at training as practical impediments. They also would like to receive assistance for strategic planning and community engagement. In addition to these obstacles above, they identified several critical gaps in funding sources and project support:

1. "Lack of financial intermediaries to facilitate access to key pools of funding such as housing tax credits, new market tax credits, and the benefits and economic development incentives available through Opportunity Zones designations;
2. Difficulties in financing pre-development costs through the lengthy funding approval period, and compliance with project requirements;
3. Lack of information flows as a result of intentional political gatekeeping;
4. Lack of data, applied research, and information to document community needs, to elaborate proposals, and for project monitoring and evaluation" (Borges-Méndez 2020).

The experience of local CDCs with federal affordable housing and community development programs offers a foundation for scaling up nonprofit sector participation in disaster recovery programs. Findings from the Borges-Méndez (2020) study indicate that there is a disconnection between local implementation of disaster recovery programs and CDCs with experience developing federally-funded housing and economic development programs. Collectively, these organizations have limited experience with recovery programs and require organizational capacity building to become competitive in the submission of proposals, and in the implementation and management of the projects. Yet a fraction of them already have a proven track record of project completion and are overcoming barriers to expand their participation in disaster recovery programs.

Policy, CDBG-DR Program Implementation, and Disaster Governance Models

In contrast to the example of ARRA stimulus funding presented earlier, we have documented that current recovery funding policy in Puerto Rico largely excludes nonprofit developers. Puerto Rico's policy programs for disaster recovery are centralized into two agencies: the Puerto Rico Department of Housing (PRDOH) for the allocation of CDBG-DR and CDBG-MIT funding, and the Central Office of Recovery, Reconstruction and Resiliency (COR3) for the management of FEMA-funded programs. In a study included in this volume and sponsored by the Center for Puerto Rican Studies, Torres Cordero (2020) asserts that these two agencies function independently of each other and, in comparison to other U.S. jurisdictions, centralize decision-making, while the implementation of programs is restricting municipal and nonprofit sector participation in publicly sponsored reconstruction projects. The conventional practice in most states is to integrate reconstruction programs under one agency and set up governance structures that promote interagency collaboration and coordination with federal agencies and are more inclusive of local governments and nonprofit organizations. In light of these circumstances, Torres Cordero asserts that "current federal guidelines for the use of CDBG-DR funds allow for a certain measure of discretion and interpretation that the Government of Puerto Rico can elect to exercise or not in order to develop more equitable programs aimed at producing a better and more just recovery" (2020, 200).

Torres Cordero (2020) identified governance models in jurisdictions affected by hurricanes with experience managing federal disaster programs and a collection of practices that foster local involvement and equitable access to resources and programs. Case studies for CDBG-DR governance models in Puerto Rico, Louisiana, South Carolina, Florida, and Texas provide specific examples of local structural arrangements and policies that support local participation and build nonprofit organizations' capacity for community and economic development. Though the mechanisms for more inclusive participation vary, examples of local policy implementation within current federal law include:

- subrecipient agreements to provide direct allocations to local governments (Louisiana, post-hurricanes Gustav and Ike, 2008);
- multiple local grantees including partnerships with nonprofit housing developers and community development corporations (South Carolina, post-Hurricane Joaquin, 2015);
- regional differentiation through RFPs and joint ventures and partnerships between government

agencies and for-profit and nonprofit organizations (Florida, post-Hurricane Irma, 2017); and
- supplemental action planning and amendments to the action plan to redistribute resources from the state to county and city levels (Texas, post-Hurricane Harvey, 2017).

Evidently, these examples highlight potential policy reforms in Puerto Rico that will lead to more inclusive practices for municipalities and nonprofit organizations. All these reforms are within the authority of the governor of Puerto Rico. Torres Cordero (2020, 220) concludes the study with a call to action:

> The maneuvers referenced in this study are by no means easy to implement and might require significant structural and programmatic changes to the ways that disaster recovery is managed and resourced. The decision is not whether to change or not—the fact or reality is that change is inevitable. The decision is how to change in a manner that is equitable and that leads to a just recovery. The cases examined here show that incremental changes are possible; however, awareness and coalition building are crucial first steps toward the design and implementation of more inclusive and equitable policies. Further, what cannot be immediately changed, can be brought to light—and casting such a light on policy failures in clear and descriptive terms is a necessary precursor to change.

Conclusions and Recommendations

Post-disaster planning and federal funding for economic recovery offer Puerto Rico a unique window of opportunity—to restore its economy and infrastructure in a more resilient fashion. However, such an opportunity hinges on local participation to join government efforts in planning and then executing a comprehensive reconstruction and recovery program. Our main goal with this volume of *CENTRO Journal* is to provide an assessment of local participation in the economic recovery of Puerto Rico. The studies included in this volume provide an assessment of businesses and the nonprofit and municipal sectors' participation in the economic recovery of Puerto Rico to date, and the contingencies such as more inclusionary policies and capacity- building initiatives that may shape such participation in the future.

But nonprofit and grassroots organizing efforts are confronted with the challenge of how to build capacity to be able to take advantage of the window of opportunity provided by the reconstruction process and disaster recovery programs.

Findings from the aforementioned studies indicate that the nonprofit and business sectors had a wide participation in the immediate emergency phase of the post-disaster recovery, primarily supported by private donations and investments, with minimal support from the local or federal government. We also saw grassroot efforts for reconstruction and community resilience, such as the CAMs, that integrates natural disaster and social reconstruction. But nonprofit and grassroots organizing efforts are confronted with the challenge of how to build capacity to be able to take advantage of the window of opportunity provided by the reconstruction process and disaster recovery programs. Their capacity to participate in the post-disaster economic recovery phase hereon is constrained due to the limited experience in the sector with housing and economic development, and mitigation and resiliency-building programs, which constitute the focus of the long-term post-disaster federal economic recovery programs.

In this context, federal recovery programs implementation, and more specifically recovery funding policy, have resulted in the outright exclusion or minimal participation of nonprofit developers in publicly-sponsored reconstruction projects in Puerto Rico to date.

The recent awards for housing rehabilitation and reconstruction were solely awarded to the private sector, with 62 percent of the contracts awarded to foreign corporations. In contrast, CDCs and nonprofit developers demonstrated that, when given the opportunity during the ARRA program, they were able to build more than 3,000 units of housing using the LIHTC program and surpassed the number of housing units built by the for-profit sector. The Torres Cordero (2020) study introduces concrete examples of policies implemented in other jurisdictions benefiting from CDBG-DR and other federal disaster programs that are more equitable by supporting inclusiveness of local governments and nonprofit organizations.

These general findings from the studies included in this volume serve as a foundation for policy and community strategies recommendations.

Policy Reform

1. Enact local inclusionary policy reforms consistent with federal disaster recovery programs to support decentralization and municipal participation, and nonprofit developers and CDCs participation. These policies include subrecipient agreements to provide direct allocations to municipalities, promoting partnerships with nonprofit housing developers and community development corporations, regional differentiation through RFPs and joint ventures and partnerships between government agencies, for-profit and nonprofit organizations, and supplemental action planning and amendments to the action plan to redistribute resources from the state to county and city levels.
2. Development of a low-cost, high-risk predevelopment fund to support existing CDCs with some experience in housing and other community development activities. In addition to subsidizing predevelopment costs, CDCs require technical support for submitting competitive proposals to FEMA, CDBG-DR, and other economic recovery targeted funding, as well as for the combination of such funds with other traditional community development programs such as housing tax credits, new market tax credits, USDA programs, and opportunity zones.

Organizational Capacity-Building

3. Development of supports for non-profits to become CDCs though professional development for current staff on housing and community economic development, for understanding federal funding for economic recovery, and for partnerships with established CDCs or other intermediaries for implementing projects.
4. Development of professional training for post-disaster economic recovery that will be delivered as comprehensive continuing education courses, via online or other structured seminars.

Industry Ecosystem

5. Strengthening community development intermediaries to provide technical assistance to nonprofit organizations and developers. In particular, Puerto Rico needs a specialized Community Development Financial Institution (CDFI) for housing, financing, and development. These financial intermediaries are important for understanding the plethora of federal programs available to nonprofit developers, including complex transactions involving syndication and the combination of funding required for most housing and commercial development projects, and the complexity of bidding, managing, and complying with federal recovery programs.
6. Creation of a hub for the exchange of information and networking to make available a directory of individuals and organizations, a calendar of activities, and opportunities for volunteerism and collaborations.
7. Creation of a data hub for easy access to interactive GIS maps available for each community and municipality in the island, to construct visualizations for community planning and contribute to crowdsourcing data efforts, and for the training of community groups on the use of the platform for community planning and development for post-disaster economic recovery.

In sum, post-disaster federal funding for economic recovery offers Puerto Rico a unique window of opportunity to restore its economy and infrastructure in a more resilient fashion while strengthening the nonprofit sector's capacity for community planning, housing development, and neighborhood revitalization. However, such an opportunity is contingent on implementing a comprehensive strategy for reforming public policy to encourage and support nonprofit developers participation in reconstruction programs, building industry capacity by strengthening intermediaries and CDCs, encouraging intra-industry partnerships and collaborations, and providing professional development for economic recovery.

NOTES

[1] FEMA's Spending Explorer, Data as of 7/31/20. Figure includes various Congressional allocations though both FEMA and SBA for Hurricanes Harvey, Irma, Maria, 2017, CA Wildfires, and other 2017 Disasters; Harvey, Irma, Maria, 2017, CA Wildfires, and other 2017 Disasters (PL 115-123); Harvey, Irma, Maria, 2017, and CA Wildfires (PL 115-156); Harvey, Irma, Maria, 2017, and CA Wildfires (PL 115-72).

[2] The IEA correlates highly with the Gross National Product and is used as an early indicator of economic activity.

[3]<?> To estimate these elements—damage, exposure, and recovery—we used 28 indicator variables in a linear discriminant analysis (LDA) to calculate the RIM index, and then classified counties into the RIM's four categories (susceptible, recovering, resilient, and usurper counties) corresponding to low, medium-low, medium-high, and high community resilience.

[4] The Charitable Sector <https://independentsector.org/about/the-charitable-sector/#:~:text=The%20nonprofit%20sector%20%E2%80%93%2010%20percent,2.7%20percent%20increase%20from%202015/>.

[5] Differences Between NGOs and Nonprofits <https://www.thebalancesmb.com/differences-between-ngos-and-nonprofits-4589762#:~:text=Nonprofits%20can%20be%20called%20non,disaster%20relief%20and%20human%20rights/>.

[6] Subtracting cooperatives that are registered as nonprofits with the IRS, which are counted as nonprofits.

[7] *Autogestión* is defined as a perspective on development and social organizing that centers peoples' right to self-determination and participation in the socioeconomic and political sphere of their communities.

[8] A social enterprise is an organization that applies commercial strategies to maximize improvements in financial, social, and environmental well-being — this may include maximizing social impact alongside profits for external shareholders. See <https://en.wikipedia.org/wiki/Social_enterprise/>.

[9] In addition, some states and state-wide associations of CDC require local certifications for local program participation. In Puerto Rico, there is no specific legal definition for CDCs at the state level, yet nonprofit organizations seeking federal funding from specific programs will need to comply with various required certifications (e.g., as CHDO or LHCA).

REFERENCES

Aldrich, D. P. 2012. *Building Resilience: Social Capital in Post-Disaster Recovery*. Chicago: University of Chicago Press.

Lobato, Manuel, Marta Álvarez and Marinés Aponte. 2020. Entrepreneurial dynamics in Puerto Rico before and after Hurricane María. *CENTRO: Journal of the Center for Puerto Rican Studies* 32(3), 39–66.

Borges-Méndez, Ramón. 2020. Community Development Corporations and Reconstruction Policy in Puerto Rico. *CENTRO: Journal of the Center for Puerto Rican Studies* 32(3), 157–98.

Comfort, L. 2007. Crisis Management in Hindsight: Cognition, Communication, Coordination, and Control. *Public Administration Review* 67, 189–97.

Correa, Pedro. 2020. FEMA approves 500-plus hazard mitigation proposals for evaluation. *The San Juan Daily Star*. Accessed 26 November 2020. <https://www.sanjuandailystar.com/post/fema-approves-500-plus-hazard-mitigation-proposals-for-evaluation/>.

COSSEC, Corporación Pública para Supervisión y Seguro de Cooperativas de Puerto Rico. 2018. Total de activos, número de socios y de empleados, por cooperativa. 30 junio. Accessed 30 August 2020. <http://www.cossec.com/cossec_new/est/Junio18/Anejo_9_Total_de_Activos,_Socios_y_Empleados_Tiempo_Completo_Por_Cooperativa_jun_2018.pdf/>.

Dyer, Christopher L. 1999. The Phoenix Effect in Post-Disaster Recovery: An Analysis of the Economic Development Administration's Culture of Response after Hurricane Andrew. In *The Angry Earth: Disaster in Sociological Perspective*, eds. A. O.-S. a. S. Hoffman. New York: Routledge.

Eller, Warren, Brian J. Gerber and Lauren E. Branch. 2015. Voluntary Nonprofit Organizations and Disaster Management: Identifying the Nature of Inter-Sector Coordination and Collaboration in Disaster Service Assistance Provision. *Risk, Hazards & Crisis in Public Policy* 6(2), 223–38.

Fadulu, Lola and Mark Walker. 2020. Trump Attaches Severe Restrictions to Puerto Rico's Long-Delayed Disaster Aid. *The New York Times* 15 January. <https://www.nytimes.com/2020/01/15/us/politics/trump-puerto-rico-disaster-aid.html/>.

Federal Emergency Management Agency (FEMA). 2017. Pre-Disaster Recovery Planning Guide for Local Governments. FEMA Publication FD 008-03, February.

________. 2018. Puerto Rico One Year after Hurricanes Irma and María. <https://www.fema.gov/news-release/2018/09/06/puerto-rico-one-year-after-hurricanes-irma-and-maria/>.

Foundation for Puerto Rico. 2019. Foundation for Puerto Rico Begins Phase One Of Whole Community Resilience Program. 15 January. Accessed 31 August 2020. <https://static1.squarespace.com/static/59e4cf35a8b2b019331ce112/t/5c3e08c203ce640330cd5e0e/1547569347160/FOUNDATION+FOR+PUERTO+RICO+BEGINS+PHASE+ONE_ENGLISH_01-15-19-converted.pdf/>.

García, Ivis and Divya Chandrasekhar. 2020. Impact of Hurricane María to the Civic Sector: A Profile of Non-Profits in Puerto Rico. *CENTRO: Journal of the Center for Puerto Rican Studies* 32(3), 67–88.

Koliou, Maria, John W. van de Lindt, Therese P. McAllister, Bruce R. Ellingwood, Maria Dillard and Harvey Cutler. 2018. State of the Research in Community Resilience: Progress and Challenges. *Sustain Resilient Infrastructure* 10.

Lam, Nina S. N., Margaret Reams, Kenan Li, Chi Li and Lillian P. Mata. 2016. Measuring Community Resilience to Coastal Hazards along the Northern Gulf of Mexico. *Natural Hazards Review* 17(1).

Luna, Emmanuel M. 2013. Community-Based Disaster Risk Reduction and Disaster Management. *Disaster Management*. 12 November. <https://doi.org/10.4324/9780203082539-15/>.

Martín, Carlos. 2018. The Evidence Based on how CDBG-DR Works for State And Local Stakeholders. Statement of Carlos Martín, Senior Fellow, Urban Institute, before the Subcommittee on Oversight and Investigations, Committee on Financial Services, United States House of Representatives. 17 May.

Meléndez, Edwin. 2020. Puerto Rico Housing and Community Development Industry's Capacity for Disaster Recovery. *CENTRO: Journal of the Center for Puerto Rican Studies* 32(3), 118–56.

Meléndez, Edwin and Lisa J. Servon. 2007. Reassessing the Role of Housing in Community-Based Urban Development. *Housing Policy Debate* 18(4), 751–83.

Mileti, Dennis S. 1999. *Disasters By Design: A Reassessment of Natural Hazards in the United States*. Washington: Joseph Henry Press.

Office of Economic Studies. 2020. The Puerto Rico Economic Activity Index ("EDB-EAI"). Economic Development Bank for Puerto Rico, September.

Patterson, O., F. Weil and K. Patel. 2010. The Role of Community in Disaster Response: Conceptual Models. *Population Research and Policy Review* 29(2), 127–41.

Peacock, Walter Gillis, Betty Hearn Morrow, and Hugh Gladwin. 1997. *Hurricane Andrew: Ethnicity, Gender, and the Sociology of Disasters*. New York: Routledge.

Red de Fundaciones de Puerto Rico. 2019. Philanthropy and Puerto Rico After Hurricane Maria: How a Natural Disaster Put Puerto Rico on the Philanthropic Map and Implications for the Future. San Juan, Puerto Rico.

Quarantelli, E. L. 1999. The disaster recovery process: What we know and do not know from research. Preliminary Paper #286. University of Delaware: Disaster Research Center.

Robinson, Scott E. and Haley Murphy. 2014. Frontiers for the Study of Nonprofit Organizations in Disasters. *Risk, Hazards & Crisis in Public Policy* 4(2), 128–34.

Severino Kathya. 2018. Rebuild Puerto Rico: A Guide to Federal Policy and Advocacy. New York: Center for Puerto Rican Studies. <https://centropr.hunter.cuny.edu/sites/default/files/data_briefs/CENTRO_POLICYGUIDE_PB2018-02.pdf/>.

Smith, Gavin and Thomas Birkland. 2012. Building a Theory of Recovery: Institutional Dimensions. *Journal of Mass Emergencies and Disasters* 3092), 147–70.

Torres Cordero, Ariam L. 2020. What Is Possible? Policy Options For Long-Term Disaster Recovery in Puerto Rico. *CENTRO: Journal of the Center for Puerto Rican Studies* 32(3), 199–223.

Villarrubia-Mendoza, Jacqueline and Roberto Vélez-Vélez. 2020. Centros de Apoyo Mutuo: reconfigurando la asistencia en tiempos de desastre. *CENTRO: Journal of the Center for Puerto Rican Studies* 32(3), 89–117.

Welsh, Mark G. and Ann-Margaret Esnard. 2009. Closing Gaps in Local Housing Recovery Planning for Disadvantaged Displaced Households. *Cityscape: A Journal of Policy Development and Research* 11(2), 195–212.

Centro Publications | 2021 CATALOGUE

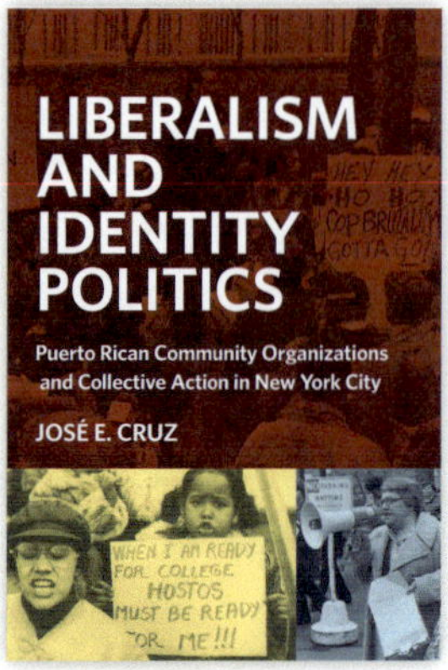

Liberalism and Identity Politics: Puerto Rican Community Organizations and Collective Action in New York City

José E. Cruz
ISBN 9781945662089 | LCCN 2017006438
$24.99; $9.99 Kindle

This book is a recollection and analysis of the role of ethnic identity in Puerto Rican community institutional development and collective action in New York City between 1960-1990. The book demonstrates that through institutional development and collective action, Puerto Ricans articulated and promoted a liberal form of identity politics in which ethnic identity and the idea of group rights provided a platform for the production of both individual and collective goods.

Not the Time to Stay: The Unpublished Plays of Víctor Fragoso

Víctor Fragoso; Edited, Translated and with an Introduction by Consuelo Martínez-Reyes
ISBN 9781945662249 | LCCN 2018034538
Pbk. 2018; 244 pages
$24.99; $9.99 Kindle

Not the Time to Stay brings to light for the first time the marvellous work of Puerto Rican playwright Víctor Fragoso. Eight plays, edited and translated by Consuelo Martínez-Reyes, portray the socio-cultural issues Fragoso sought to expose: the choice and difficulties of migration, the clash between American and Puerto Rican societies, the oppression suffered by Latinos in the USA, homelessness, and domestic violence, among others. Fragoso played a key role in the New York City theatre scene in the 1970s, and in the overall interrogation of Puerto Rican and Latino identities in the USA.

Patria: Puerto Rican Revolutionary Exiles in Late Nineteenth Century New York

Edgardo Meléndez
$24.99

Patria examines the activities and ideals of Puerto Rican revolutionaries exiles in New York City at the end of the nineteenth century. The study is centered in the writings, news reports, and announcements by and about Puerto Ricans in the newspaper *Patria*, of the Cuban Revolutionary Party. The book looks at the political, organizational and ideological ties between Cuban and Puerto Rican revolutionaries in exile, as well as the events surrounding the war of 1898. The analysis also offers a glimpse into the daily life and community of Puerto Rican exiles in late nineteenth century New York City.

FORTHCOMING

Fighting on Two Fronts: Puerto Rican Soldiers in the Korean War

Harry Franqui-Rivera
$24.99

Tens of thousands of Puerto Rican soldiers took part in the Korean War as combat troops. Many of these soldiers fought as part of the 65th U.S. Army Infantry Regiment, "el sesenta y cinco." Its men were known as the Borinqueneers. During the war, the 65th became a national icon on the island and among the growing Puerto Rican communities in the mainland. The island-based press and political figures made reference to the 65th as a catalyst for forging a modern person and a modern Puerto Rico, while the community in New York highlighted the Puerto Rican soldiers' heroic efforts and sacrifices to counter racial discrimination. The Borinqueneers helped established a bridge between New York and the island. These Puerto Rican soldiers' service required them to fight on two fronts. They fought relentlessly North Korean and Chinese soldiers in fierce combat. They also fought brutal racial discrimination within the U.S. Armed Forces. Their story is a neglected chapter in the history of the Puerto Ricans.

Centro Publications | 2021 CATALOGUE

Race, Front and Center: Perspectives on Race Among Puerto Ricans

Edited by Carlos Vargas-Ramos
ISBN 9781945662003
LCCN 2016030601. Pbk. 2017; 403 pages
$24.99

Race, Front and Center is a collection of essays that captures in a single volume the breadth of research on the subject of race among Puerto Ricans, both in Puerto Rico, in the United States and in the migration between the two countries. Its twenty-two chapters divided into seven sections address the intellectual, aesthetic and historical trajectories that have served to inform the creation of a national identity among Puerto Ricans and how race as a social identity fits into the process of national identity-building.

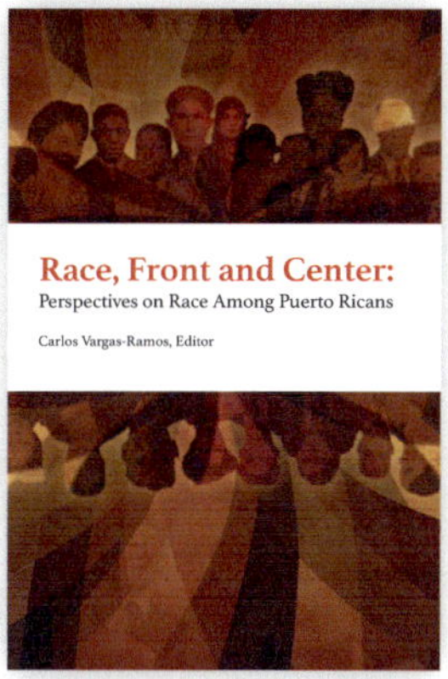

Before the Wave: Puerto Ricans in Philadelphia, 1910–1945

Víctor Vázquez-Hernández
ISBN 9781945662027
LCCN 2016047262. Pbk. 2017; 129 pages
$19.99

This book recounts the genesis of the Puerto Rican community in Philadelphia during the interwar years (1917–1945). It connects the origins of this community to the mass migration of the post-WW II years when Puerto Ricans consolidated their presence in Philadelphia (1945–1985). This study compares the experiences of Puerto Ricans with that of the Italians, the Polish, and African Americans in Philadelphia during the early twentieth century.

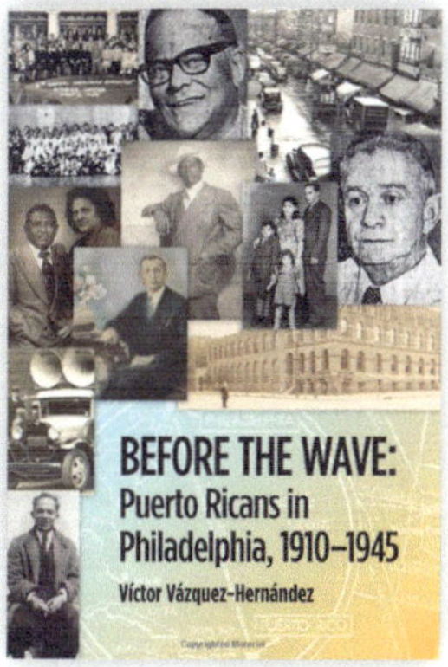

Rhythm & Power: Performing Salsa in Puerto Rican and Latino Communities

Edited by Derrick León Washington, Priscilla Renta and Sydney Hutchinson
ISBN 9781945662164
LCCN 2017038687. Pbk. 2017; 88 pages
$12.00

The story of New York salsa is one of cultural fusion, artistry, and skilled marketing. A multi-disciplinary collective of scholars illuminate how immigrant and migrant communities in New York City—most notably from Puerto Rico—nurtured and developed salsa, growing it from a local movement playing out in the city's streets and clubs into a global phenomenon.

State of Puerto Ricans 2017

Edited by Edwin Meléndez
and Carlos Vargas-Ramos
ISBN 9781945662126
LCCN 2017021705. Pbk. 2017; 138 pages
$20.00

This book provides an updated overview of some of the most salient subjects and themes about the Puerto Rican population in the United States at present. It highlights the continued mobility and expansion of the Puerto Rican population throughout the country, including state-to-state migration, migration from Puerto Rico in light of the economic crisis in the island, as well as the role of service in the armed forces in anchoring new areas of settlement.

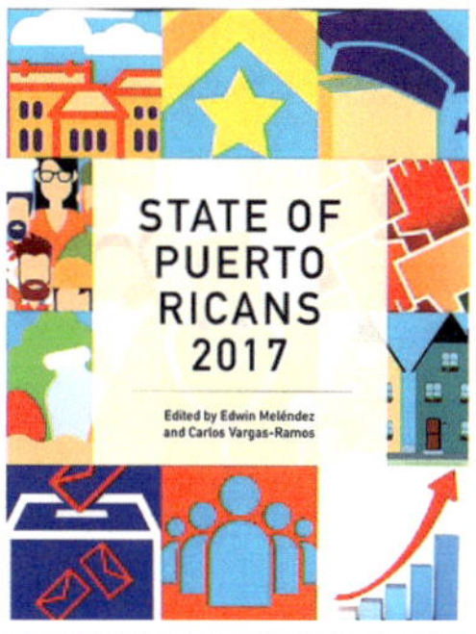

Centro Publications | 2021 CATALOGUE

Almanac of Puerto Ricans in the United States

Editors Jennifer Hinojosa and
Carlos Vargas-Ramos
ISBN 978-1945662072
LCCN 2017002040. Pbk. 2016; 167 pages.
$20

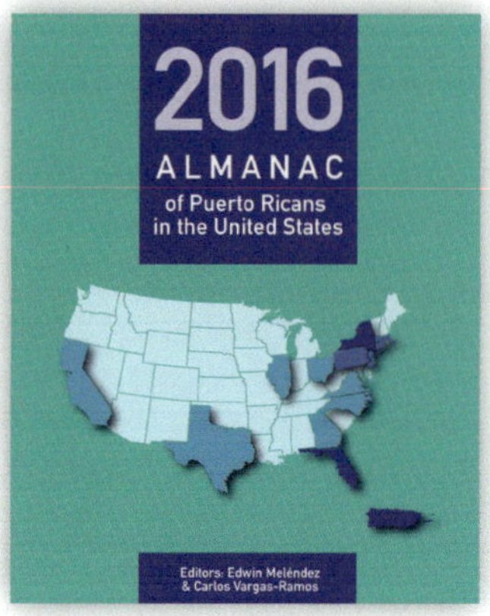

Learn more about the recent changes in the Puerto Rican community on the mainland United States through national and state-specific demographic data. The almanac compiles information on social, economic, and civic conditions of the Puerto Rican population in nine key states, and includes maps, tables, and descriptions of the population nationwide.

The Bodega: A conerstone of Puerto Rican Barrios (The Justo Martí Collection)

Carlos Sanabria
ISBN 978-1945662065. Pbk. 2016; 43 pages.
$15

This photo book is a compilation of photographs of bodegas in 1960s New York City shot by Cuban photographer Justo Martí. The photos are part of Centro's Justo Martí collection, which documents the life and activities of the individuals, families and organizations that made up the Puerto Rican experience in New York.

Gilberto Gerena Valentín: My Life as a Community Activist, Labor Organizer, and Progressive Politician in NYC

Edited by Carlos Rodríguez Fraticelli; Translated by Andrew Hurley;
With an Introduction by José E. Cruz
ISBN 9781878483744; 2013; 315 pages.
$20

Gilberto Gerena Valentín is a key figure in the development of the Puerto Rican community in the United States, especially from the forties through the seventies. He was a union organizer, community leader, political activist and general in the war for the civil-rights recognition of his community. In his memoirs, Gilberto Gerena Valentín takes us into the center of the fierce labor, political, civil-rights, social and cultural struggles waged by Puerto Ricans in New York from the 1940s through the 1970s.

Puerto Ricans at the Dawn of the New Millennium

Edited by Edwin Meléndez
and Carlos Vargas-Ramos
ISBN 978187848379-9. Pbk. 2014; 319 pages.
$24.99

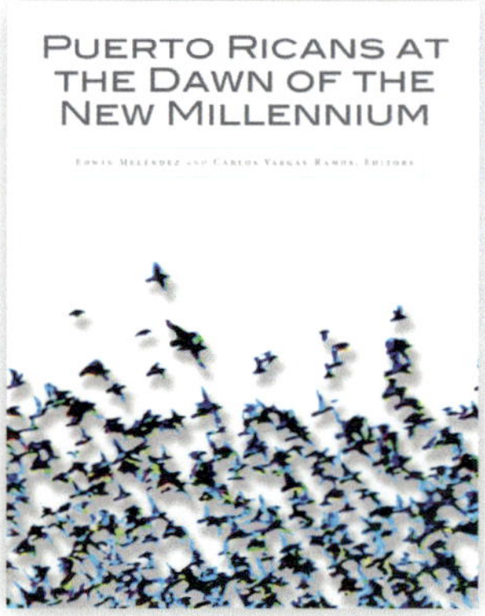

This edited volume features chapters by Centro researchers and outside scholars presenting new research on social, economic, political and health conditions of the Puerto Rican population in the United States and highlighting the improvements and the challenges in this rapidly changing and growing community.

Centro Publications | 2021 CATALOGUE

Soy Gilberto Gerena Valentín: memorias de un puertorriqueño en Nueva York

Gilberto Gerena Valentín; Edición de Carlos Rodríguez Fraticelli
ISBN: 9781878483645—ISBN: 9781878483454 (ebook); 2013; 302 pages.
$20 (print); $6 (ebook)

Gilberto Gerena Valentín es uno de los personajes claves en el desarrollo de la comunidad puertorriqueña en Nueva York. En sus memorias, Gilberto Gerena Valentín nos lleva al centro de las continuas luchas sindicales, políticas, sociales y culturales que los puertorriqueños fraguaron en Nueva York durante el periodo de la Gran Migración hasta los años setenta.

The AmeRícan Poet: Essays on the Work of Tato Laviera

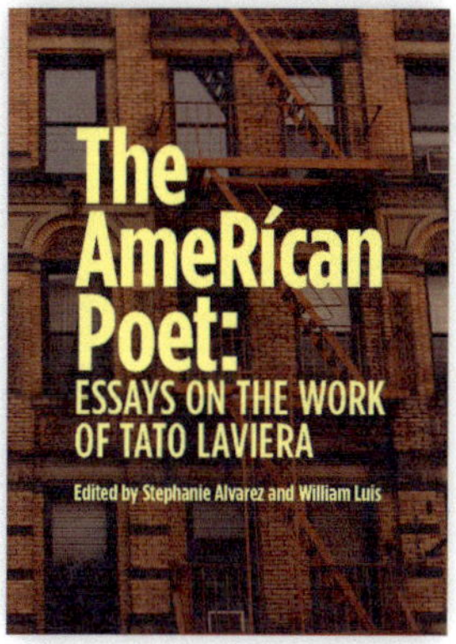

Edited by Stephanie Alvarez and William Luis
ISBN: 9781878483669; 2014. Pbk. 2014; 418 pages.
$24.99

A collection of thirteen essays, an introduction and a foreword by fifteen established and emerging scholars. The essays discuss diverse aspects of Laviera's life and substantial body of work that includes five published collections of poetry, twelve written and staged plays, and many years of political, social, literary and healthcare activism. The book also includes four unpublished poems and the play King of Cans.

The Stories I Read to the Children: The Life and Writing of Pura Belpré, the Legendary Storyteller, Children's Book Author, and New York Public Librarian

Pura Belpré; Edited and Biographical Introduction by Lisa Sánchez González
ISBN: 9781878483805—ISBN: 9781878483454 (Kindle). 2013; 286 pages.
$20 (print); $7.99 (Kindle)

The Stories I Read to the Children documents, for the very first time, Pura Belpré's contributions to North American, Caribbean, and Latin American literary and library history. Thoroughly researched but clearly written, this study is scholarship that is also accessible to general readers, students, and teachers. Lisa Sánchez González has collected, edited, and annotated over 40 of Belpré's stories and essays, most of which have never been published. Her introduction to the volume is the most extensive study to date of Belpré's life and writing.

The State of Puerto Ricans 2013

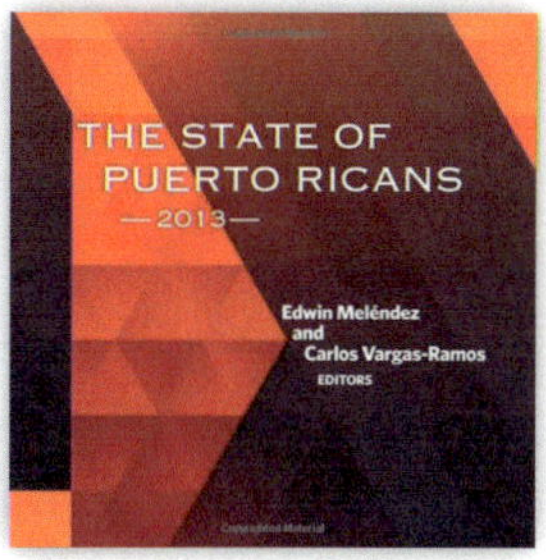

Edited by Edwin Meléndez
and Carlos Vargas-Ramos
ISBN: 9781878483720; 2013; 91 pages.
$15
The State of Puerto Ricans 2013 collects in a single report the most current data on social, economic and civic conditions of the Puerto Rican population in the United States available from governmental sources, mostly the U.S. census Bureau.

Celebrating 45 Years of Achievements

The Center for Puerto Rican Studies (Centro) has grown considerably over the past forty-five years, fine-tuning our research, archives, pedagogy, and programming so as to evolve with the times. This guide provides an overview of the history and achievements of Centro since its founding in 1973, and a summary of the programs and educational tools available to the public.

https://bit.ly/2KnYXXp
https://centropr.hunter.cuny.edu/centrovoices/current-affairs/celebrating-45-years-guide-centro

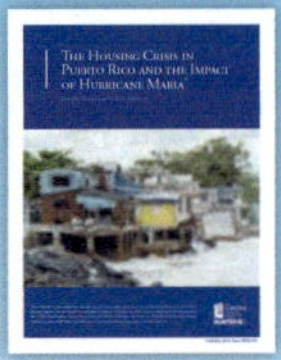

The Housing Crisis in Puerto Rico and the Impact of Hurricane Maria

By all counts, Puerto Rico's housing market is in a deep and prolonged crisis. At least 18 percent of Puerto Rico's housing stock is vacant as a result of the island's prolonged economic recession. This report examines the housing crisis which commenced in 2006, and how the spike in foreclosures after Hurricane Maria suggests that vacant units are increasing at an accelerated rate.

https://goo.gl/eTZG2Y
https://centropr.hunter.cuny.edu/research/data-center/research-briefs/housing-crisis-puerto-rico-and-impact-hurricane-maria

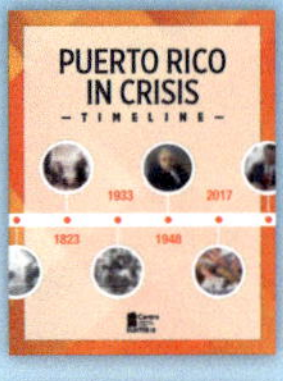

Puerto Rico in Crisis Timeline

Since 2006 Puerto Rico has been facing an unprecedented economic and fiscal crisis that shows little signs of ending or abating in the foreseeable future. In this timeline, we summarize the most important milestones and turning points since 1898, and the impacts that United States and local policies have had on Puerto Rico's Economy.

https://bit.ly/2lGZuvl
https://centropr.hunter.cuny.edu/education/puerto-rico-crisis-timeline

Rebuild Puerto Rico: A Guide to Federal Policy and Advocacy

The impact of Hurricane Maria will be felt for decades, and long-term recovery and rebuilding efforts in Puerto Rico are expected to take years. This report provides an overview of federal disaster relief policy, dissects the recovery process and the role of federal assistance, and discusses possible entry points for advocacy efforts.

https://goo.gl/7rKUa9
https://centropr.hunter.cuny.edu/events-news/rebuild-puerto-rico/policy/rebuild-puerto-rico-guide-federal-policy-and-advocacy

Puerto Rico: Two Years After Hurricane Maria (September 2019)

In this report we provide a continuation of lasts years' timeline of the major occurrences in the aftermath, an analysis of the media's coverage of the disaster, the impact of Hurricane Maria Evacuees on the Puerto Rican population in the Unites States and the migration effects resulting in school closures.

https://bit.ly/2nW5Vfh
https://centropr.hunter.cuny.edu/research/data-center/research-briefs/puerto-rico-two-years-after-hurricane-maria

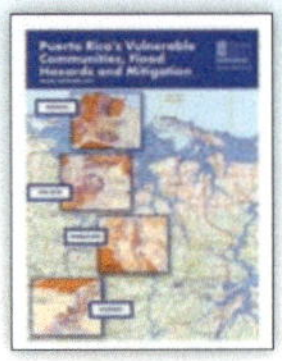

Puerto Rico's Vulnerable Communities and Flood Hazards and Mitigation (forthcoming)

Using the 2017 U.S. Census Bureau's American Community Survey (5-year estimates), at least 15% of Puerto Rico's population resided in the 100-year floodplain. This report utilizes the Center for Disease Control's (CDC) 'social vulnerability index' (SVI) to measure resiliency among the Island's communities faced with human or natural induced hazards, like flooding. The purpose of this research brief is to help inform policy, planners, and community leaders the population and housing structures at risk in the Island's floodplains.

Nonprofit Sector's Capacity for Disaster Recovery in Puerto Rico (forthcoming)

Post-disaster planning and federal funding for economic recovery offer Puerto Rico's community development industry a unique window of opportunity. This opportunity hinges on the capacity of the nonprofit sector securing federal grants, joining government efforts in planning and then executing economic development projects. This report provides an evidence-based assessment of the current capacity of and prospects for the nonprofit sector to become an active participant in the economic recovery of Puerto Rico and, more generally, to be able take advantage of this window of opportunity.

The Center for Puerto Rican Studies (Centro) is the nation's leading university-based institution devoted to the interdisciplinary study of the Puerto Rican experience in the United States. Centro is dedicated to understanding, preserving and sharing the Puerto Rican experience in the United States. Centro invites Centro Voices contributors to make use of the extensive archival, bibliographic and research material preserved in its Library and Archives.

The Centro Library and Archives is devoted to collecting, preserving and providing access to resources documenting the history and culture of Puerto Ricans. The Centro Library and Archives was established in 1973 as a component of the Center for Puerto Rican Studies. The collections include books, current and historic newspapers and periodicals, audio, film & video, manuscripts, photographs, art prints, and recorded music. The Library and Archives provides services and programs to the scholarly community as well as the general public. Constituents are diverse and come from the United States and abroad. The Library and Archives facilitates access to information on its holdings through the City University's online public catalog or CUNY+. It also provides research and information assistance via phone and email.

Center for Puerto Rican Studies, Hunter College, CUNY
695 Park Avenue, New York, NY | 212-772-5688 | centropr.hunter.cuny.edu

Centro
CENTER FOR PUERTO RICAN STUDIES
HUNTER CUNY The City University of New York

Made in United States
Cleveland, OH
05 November 2026

47664965R00019